Carol Ann Duffy
Poet Laureate
Introduction

Gillian Clarke
Museum of Zoology
Archaeopteryx

Daljit Nagra
Museum of Archaeology
and Anthropology
*The Museum of Archaeology
and Anthropology in Cambridge*

Ann Gray
Botanic Garden
Pressing Beauty

Imtiaz Dharker
Cambridge University Library
When the copperplate cracks

Owen Sheers
Fitzwilliam Museum
Turn

Sean B
Museum
Nike of

Matthe
The Sed
of Earth
Animal

Jo Shapcott
The Polar Museum
Fox Collar

Don Paterson
Whipple Museum of
the History of Sciences
A Pocket Horizon

Jackie Kay
Kettle's Yard
The House of Juxta-Positions

CW00406798

Thresholds

Poets in residence
at the University of Cambridge
museums and collections.

This anthology of poems was born out of the Thresholds project, a poetry and museums project supported by the University of Cambridge and Arts Council England in Cambridge Museums and Collections.

I invited ten of the best UK poets writing today to take part in an unprecedented and extraordinary series of residencies at the University of Cambridge.

Each poet spent time in their museum or collection exploring the collections and working with young people, helping them to develop their critical thinking skills as well as their writing. They were also commissioned to write a poem inspired and informed by the collections. Most of the Thresholds poets went on to write more than one poem, some have written a sequence and others are working towards a collection. This anthology contains all the commissioned poems.

Seamus Heaney once said, 'Poetry is more a threshold than a path, one constantly departed from, at which readers and writers undergo, in their different ways, the experience of being at the same time summoned and released'.

The Thresholds project summoned hundreds of people to poetry between November 2012 and May 2013, and to these many remarkable and beautiful museums and collections through events, exciting interventions, online discussions and new writing. So let me invite you to cross the threshold into this wonderful anthology and encourage you to visit the collections which inspired the poems.

Carol Ann Duffy
Poet Laureate

Museum of Zoology
Gillian Clarke

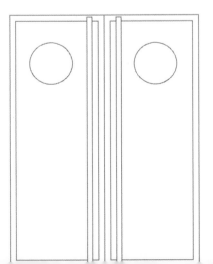

Archaeopteryx
from 'Behind Glass'

The first bird in the world
stilled in stony silence behind glass.
Flight feathers, wishbone, that perching foot,
found in the limestone of a salt lagoon, a mould
from the Jurassic, print, exactitude,
a frozen moment in Earth's book of stone,
the transition between dinosaur and bird,
a memory of wing-feathers, skull and bones,
like the impression left by a magpie on the lawn,
bump-landing, lift-off, touch and go,
its wing-beats leaving angels in the snow
an icy hour before dawn.
                  First bird,
thence every warbler, song-thrush, wren,
the blackbird in the ash, five notes repeating
                        again, again, again.

Museum of Archaeology and Anthropology
Daljit Nagra

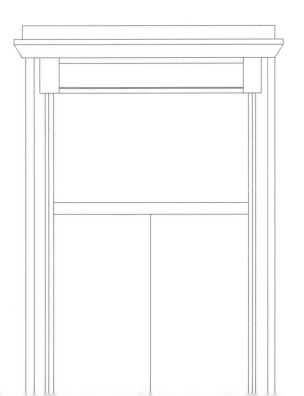

The Museum of Archaeology and Anthropology in Cambridge

I am held apologetically in a seminar room.
This is the dawn of my days as a poet-in-residence
who has been commissioned to produce a poem.
My host furnishes me with an apple strudel slice.

Yesterday, my slice was one upon many settled before
the Prime Minister of Fiji who was visiting his island's wares.
I overhear our tyrant was not exposed to the 'cannibal forks'.
But was most impressed by the kava bowl and whale

teeth whose curves he stroked with gloveless hands
before being won by a slice of the sweetest English apples . . .

Botanic Garden
Ann Gray

Pressing Beauty
Cambridge University Herbarium

We're pressing flowers. Beth tightens screws
until the buttercup is bleeding yellow. I want
her to have the names, the magic that starts:
Archangel, Bugle, Corncockle, Mayweed,
Toadflax to Wolf's Bane, the count of petals,
where we found them, the month and weather –
first buttercup, in the wind and rain, long field,
February, Cornwall. Bees like yellow. We draw
a bee. Dried stalks of things fall out of all my books:
Alhambra, Granada, a dark rose, its scent long gone,
and a note that says – *June, hot and thirsty, golden fish*
in a long pond, the moon falls as stars through the ceilings.
Water Crowfoot, Goats Rue, Bedstraw. Lady's Smock,
vanilla touched with mauve, lilac – *Churchbridge,*
the field is full of them, a pale lake pulling at the throat
of May. Blackthorn. That page is torn. Dogrose, a smear
of blood. *July* – Foxglove, fat and speckled, badly
squashed. Gorse, no cloying smell but the colour
of sun blazing. A grandmother should have secrets,
share them. We take two 2lb weights that sit beside
my scales, talk of patience, a space of time, how they'll
change, how we'll have to close our eyes to see them,
because this isn't science. We're pressing beauty.

Cambridge
University Library
Imtiaz Dharker

When the copperplate cracks
Theatrum orbis terrarum

So this is how it is done, one hand inching
round the coast to map its ins and outs,
to mark the point where ink may kiss
the river's mouth, or blade make up
a *terra incognita*, an imagined south.

This is where the needle turns to seek
a latitude, where acid bites the naked shore
and strips the sea till it is nothing
more than metallic light. The lived terrain
comes face to face with its mirror image

on the page, the world made up
and made again from sheets of ore, slept in,
loved in, tumbled, turned until the copper
buckles. You see it clearly in the print,
the place where metal

has been wounded, mended, where the hand
attempts to heal the breakline in the heart.

Fitzwilliam Museum
Owen Sheers

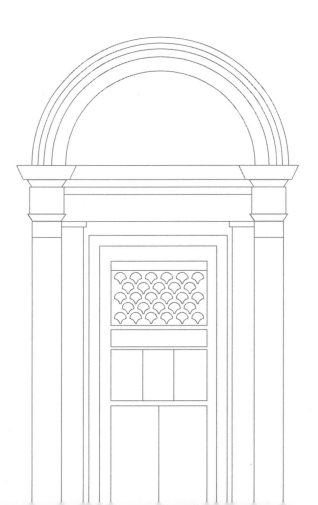

Turn

from 'Working at the Edge of Loss: Poems of the Fitzwilliam'
Piece of limestone with drawing of reindeer, c.13,000–12,000 BC

At first glance no more than an ochre flake,
a skimming stone that might have been picked,
fitting so well as it would

into the 'C' of thumb and forefinger,
to be launched, a stuttering ellipsis,
into the heart of the river.

But look what we'd lose if it had.
This reindeer, alive in the lines
of its haunch, neck and hoof,

scratch-shaded above the suggestion of a sheath,
its motionless movement
etched by a burin struck from flint.

You might have walked past it, most did.
But not you.
You caught it, here in the forest, in this stone.

You saw the truth in the turn of its head
which seems to look back, out of this case
into the galleries of Egypt and Rome

and then further still,
into the rooms of portraits and sculpture
and on again through the walls altogether

only to taper in the city's outer streets
at a bedsit where a student leans over her desk
to draw an arrow across her screen

and make a mark in light.

All this it seems to say in the turn of its head.
All this which lies behind me
all this which I am moving towards,
all this, is my herd, my legacy.

Museum of Classical
Archaeology
Sean Borodale

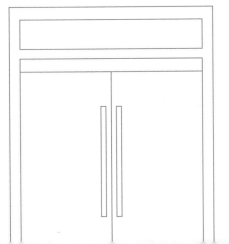

Nike of Paionios in Plaster of Paris

Most are austere, fragmented, absorbed in a wound,
locked to a mirror in a mirror.
Musicians go first, with the old, or the lame,
but there is no sound.
It's like a mime, held breath, Helios.

We have to stand dedicating lengths of *our* time
as they survive, mutely as we do, in photos or death.
Lifted from Hades' struggling shadow
they have all turned pale

in wedding-cake-white, bony cement.

Like animals on the ark, they must be thirsty
in uniform plaster; oddly supported on crutches, thin air,
utterly breakable.

Nike, for instance, a shattered array of mid-air wing,
tampered by event;
I am ruined with her, air-franked apart.
But it's the face, blown-off, nearest, and the hissing bit of
breathless lung,
like a breathing she has to lift from the stomach.
It does not self-repair, this kind of damage.

And it's quarantine here, for mysteries and illness
and visitors slowed right down to time-lapse like us.
She is our idea;
a residual instant of a tide-mark's remnant.

Her light is a kind of glue; our shared time is warped.

The Sedgwick Museum
of Earth Sciences
Matthew Hollis

Animal

Earth woke you at an unshook rib.
We had no books to base you on,

we had no tools to pare you down,
so incomplete,

you were both catalogue and kit,
the takings of a varied ground:

carpals from the marl pits,
grasses grown through a jaw bone.

All bones became your bones.
We laid fibula to femur,

radius to humerus,
one hip crocked from female, one of male;

our ivory, uncommon kid,
from such modesty you stood.

Light wounded, wind wounded.
Water slipped from your sternum.

You pined for the forest floor,
you pined for your own kind;

but there were no kinds like yours:
so bit-part, out of epoch,

mocked by those from nearer shore.
We took them on and knocked them down –

damned if they cast pity on your name –
and wondered

what kind of kindness this could be,
to leave you where you could be left,

unwarranted to all but us;
circling at your roof of fire and straw.

Night moves at the welter pools.
The summer slips, the winter hoars.

Eleven times the long hand crosses short;
we go so far.

One day the rings will slip from our fingers.
But not from yours. Everything

we almost are we lose. My animal,
you cannot know how hard in love you are.

The Polar Museum
Jo Shapcott

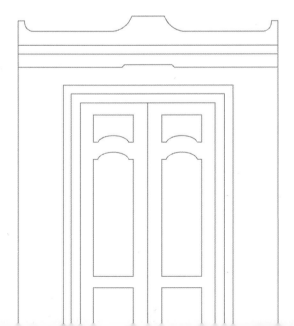

Fox Collar

First, catch yer fox with a gripping trap,
one made all of iron, with enough clickets
to hold her but not to crush her leg.
You will do well to bury it under an inch of snow,
put meat in, and meat juices about the place.
Many fur-bearing creatures make a go of it up here,
but fox is best for what we want, with her speed,
with her thick, thick white fur all over
and on her soles, too, her roundy body,
all upholstered for the cold. She go far north,
she do. She is bold and will take the trap.
I heard how one grabbed seal meat
from under the bonce of a midshipman,
right there, in his tent, a fool who guarded chow
by making it his pillow. They was all
blizzed in. He set off an ice quake
running after she, with his blubber toes
and his lost dreams of big heaps to eat.

You got your collar, we brung eight, will
use them all, good leather, fitted
to an English fox back home for size.
You got your engraving tools, so scribe
careful thus: *HBMS ENTERPRISE WQ*
(you won't fit Winter Quarters in long)
LAT 71.35 N LONG 117.39 W XX XII 1851.
Grasp her by the scruff, don't free her
from the trap till the collar's on firm.
Watch her run, maybe with a wobble
in her gait from where the iron bit.
But it won't bother her much
as she goes off and off, with her big eye,
and her empty guts, maybe a hundred
maybe more miles on a hunt and a flyer
with fur feet which make the snow and ice
just a game for her, though it do murder us.

Whipple Museum of
the History of Sciences
Don Paterson

A Pocket Horizon

The idea, I guess, is on the kind of day
the vapours are sent down to blind and choke us
one still might gain some distance, much the way
this shotglass seems to give me a little focus
or this stone in my shoe some foothold on events.
Its disc of jet on three gold screws would do
for a doll's house table at a doll's house séance.
I'm trying to what exactly. Level with you?

Chin down on the bar-rail and one-eyed
to get it true and straight and down to scale.
But my huge head looms above its tiny tide
and my breath is screaming like a winter gale
I think there's no one on the other side
O love, where is my white or my black sail

Kettle's Yard
Jackie Kay

The House of Juxta-Positions
The Dining Table

Let's not get bogged down here.
Here is a table. A table in an art house;
not an art-house table. This table
sailed the triangular route
and heard the cries of the damned.
This table, made of beech wood,
numb, helpless, thick as a plank,
witnessed the jumps, the suicide-
escapes into the lost Atlantic; the crossings
where grief, guns, copper, coffee, Rum,
tobacco, sugar, slaves were carried over.
This table stood, cells in the wood.
And none of it could be understood.

Is it to make us think, this dining table
in this beautifully composed house?
Is it a sort of joke? Blood and ink stains
just the same? As if to hint that pain
comes from the same place as art?
And only art can redress time?
How could Helen and Jim sit, of an evening,
in this lovely space with the last light:
the lemon on the plate, Miro's balance,
eating supper off this ballast?
Not a rock or stone or pebble here;
not a great painting, not a work of art, well made,
says it's fine to dine off the slave trade.

The House of Juxta-Positions
Helen's Room

Not too late, then, to catch the blessed light
through the eyes of *The Radar* in this winter sun;
to see the past and present side by side;
to take your hand once again,
walk into the bitter biting wind.
The key turns on what we don't understand.
Every joy is twinned
With an opposite: a hinterland –
I've been in Helen's room,
A phrase to coin: happiness
reframed in the dark afternoon.
Not too late to know that as soon
As something was here once, it's gone.

Not too late, in the House of Juxtapositions,
where Scotland and England meet, old friends,
to remember that last conversation
Might last to the nether land.
Here, where strangers pair, maps are bilinear;
balance acts, echoes matter;
stones, pebbles, shells, statues;
the great art of fractured crockery;
the democracy of light and dark.
Not too late to see the beauty in broken things:
that cracks can visibly mend;
the painted flowers can grow.
Love in separate rooms,
Single beds, matching spreads.

Not too late to allow Winifred to take you
past the daffodils, the Norman window
through the canvas, out to the churchyard . . .
the backdoor of Kettle's Yard,
Where Helen and Jim walked
the path of the waiting graves;
remembering what you knew.
The old stones painted by light;
the last of the sun on the cobbled path.
Not too late to hear the song in your head,
that whistles whatever darkness lies ahead.
Not too late to hear the music of the blessed.